USA TODAY
CULTURAL MOSAIC

The Asian Pacific American Experience

Karen Sirvaitis

Twenty-First Century Books · Minneapolis

This book takes a broad look at Asian Pacific Americans. However, like all cultural groups, the Asian Pacific American community is extremely diverse. Each member of the community relates to his or her background and heritage in different ways, and each has had a different experience of what it means to be Asian Pacific American.

Twenty-First Century Books
A division of Lerner Publishing Group, Inc.
241 First Avenue North
Minneapolis, MN 55401 U.S.A.

Website address: www.lernerbooks.com

Library of Congress Cataloging-in-Publication Data

Sirvaitis, Karen, 1961–
The Asian Pacific American experience / by Karen Sirvaitis.
p. cm. – (USA TODAY cultural mosaic)
Includes bibliographical references and index.
ISBN 978-0-7613-4089-8 (lib. bdg. : alk. paper)
1. Asian Americans—History—Juvenile literature. 2. Asian Americans—Social life and customs—Juvenile literature. I. Title.
E184.A75S57 2011
973'.0495–dc22 2009045925

Manufactured in the United States of America
1 - DP - 7/15/10

Young dancers dressed in kimonos, the traditional Japanese attire, perform at the Japantown Summer Festival in San Francisco, California.

INTRODUCTION:

ASIANS AND PACIFIC ISLANDERS IN AMERICA

Asia is the largest continent in the world. It stretches from the Arctic Ocean in the north to the Indian Ocean in the south. Asia shares a border with Europe to the west. Asia's eastern border is the Pacific Ocean. Within this wide expanse of sea lie tens of thousands of Pacific Islands. These islands include Hawaii, a U.S. state.

Asians have a very long history in America. Fifteen thousand years ago, groups of Asians crossed a land bridge that once connected Siberia in northeastern Asia with Alaska in North America. They became the ancestors of modern-day Native Americans. The waters of the Bering Sea eventually covered the land bridge, ending Asian migration to the Americas for centuries.

Asians did not begin arriving in North America again until 1763. This time they came by ship. Several Filipino (from the Philippines) sailors were working on board Spanish trade ships. The ships docked in Acapulco, Mexico. To escape harsh conditions on the vessels, the sailors jumped ship. They made their way east to the Gulf of Mexico. In Louisiana they created a small village called Saint Malo.

Since the late 1700s, millions more Asians have crossed the ocean to come to America. The first large group of Asians in North America were Chinese. They arrived around 1848, at the start of the California gold rush. Some came to mine gold. Others took jobs building railroads. Some became farmers. In the mid-1800s, many

Asian immigrants work on the North Pacific Coast Railroad in Corte Madera, California, in 1898.

Japanese immigrants moved to Hawaii to work on sugar plantations. At the time, Hawaii was not part of the United States. From Hawaii some Japanese workers moved to California.

The early Asian immigrants worked for low wages. They faced many hardships. Non–Asian Americans often treated them harshly. From the late 1800s to the mid-1900s, the United States prohibited most Asians from entering the country. For Japanese Americans, the worst period was World War II (1939–1945). During this war, the United States and Japan were enemies. The U.S. government distrusted Japanese Americans and locked them in prison camps in the United States.

After World War II, more Asians came to the United States. They came from India, Pakistan, Korea, the Philippines, and other Asian nations. Some came for jobs or education. Others came to join relatives who had arrived earlier. In 1959 Hawaii became a U.S. state. U.S. and Hawaiian cultures became more closely linked.

The Vietnam War (1957–1975) brought violence and U.S. soldiers to the Southeast Asian nations of Vietnam, Cambodia, and Laos. After the war, many people from these countries moved to the United States.

In the twenty-first century, Asians continue to move to the United States. When they arrive, many live in neighborhoods with other people from their home countries. Some of these neighborhoods are nicknamed after the native land. Chinatown, Filipinotown, Japantown, and Little India are some examples.

The neighborhoods bustle with activity. Asian restaurants, markets, and shops line the streets. Storefronts are marked with signs printed in Asian languages. In the markets, shoppers can find Asian foods. Passersby can hear Asian Americans speaking Asian languages.

About 13.5 million Asian Pacific Americans live in the United States. They are a vital part of American society. This book will look at who they are, where they've been, and where they're going.

Chinatown in New York City is the largest Chinatown in the United States. It's common to see signs written in Chinese there.

CHAPTER 1:

CHARACTERS IN PRINT

About 60 percent of Asian Americans were born in Asia. The rest were born in the United States to Asian American parents. Those born in Asia have adapted to U.S. culture and customs. This includes learning English.

Some immigrants learned English in Asia. For instance, children in the Philippines study English in school. English is widely used in Filipino education, business, and government, along with Tagalog and other Filipino languages. In India, more than half the people speak English. Many immigrants from India already speak English well when they arrive in the United States.

But other Asian immigrants know only their native language. When they arrive in the United States, they need to learn to speak, read, and write English. Many also need to learn a new alphabet. Most Asian languages are written using characters, or symbols. Unlike letters, which stand for specific sounds, characters stand for parts of words or for ideas.

An Asian American practices writing Chinese characters in San Francisco, California. Many Asian languages use characters, or symbols, instead of letters.

LANGUAGE BARRIERS

Once in the United States, some Asian children and adults attend special schools to learn English. Many children attend only public schools, where English is the language of instruction. These children may have a hard time talking to their teachers and fellow students. Their schoolbooks and lessons are written only in English. Many Asian immigrant children do poorly in school at first because their English skills are poor.

Despite these barriers, most Asian immigrants eventually master English. Learning a new language is usually easier for children than for adults. In some Asian American families, English-speaking children translate for non-English-speaking parents. They help their parents with everyday needs, such as buying groceries, paying bills, and communicating with other Americans.

The Hula

In ancient times, Hawaiians did not have a written language. They passed on information by telling stories and singing songs. They also used dances to tell stories about nature, people, and gods. The hula is an ancient Hawaiian dance. In earlier centuries, hula dancers told stories by swaying their hips and arms. Musicians playing drums and rattles accompanied the dancers. Singers recited chants.

In modern times, the hula is still a popular dance in Hawaii. Modern hula musicians play guitars and ukuleles. Songs have replaced the chants. But hula performers still tell many of the same stories their ancestors told centuries ago.

In some parts of the United States, local governments also help non-English speakers. California has more Asian Americans than any other state. English is the state's official language, but the state government prints many forms in different Asian languages. These languages include Chinese, Korean, Tagalog, Vietnamese, and Thai. Asian immigrants who do not read English can read important information in their native languages.

USA TODAY Snapshots®

Foreign student enrollment in USA

The U.S. attracted 583,000 foreign students in the 2006-07 school year, about 4% of the nation's 15 million college students.

Countries sending the most:

Country	Students
India	83,833
China	67,723
South Korea	62,392
Japan	35,282
Taiwan	29,094

Source: Institute of International Education

By Anne R. Carey and Alejandro Gonzalez, USA TODAY, 2008

Asians continue to move to the United States for an education. In fact, Asians make up a large percentage of foreign students in the United States. Many Asian students remain in the United States permanently after graduation.

ASIAN AMERICAN LITERATURE

Many Asian Americans have written about their experiences in the United States. Their stories give readers insight into being an Asian immigrant.

In 1957 Japanese American John Okada wrote *No-No Boy*. This novel tells about the life of a Japanese American after World War II. During the war, Japanese Americans were interned, or kept in camps. The U.S. government asked them a series of questions. One question was about their loyalty to the United States. Another was about their willingness to serve in the U.S. military. Men who answered no to both questions were called no-no boys. They were

Native Speakers

About 13.5 million Asian Pacific Americans live in the United States. Most of them speak at least some English, and many of them are fluent in English. Asian Americans also speak native languages in their homes. This list shows the number of speakers for specific Asian languages in the United States:

Chinese: 2.2 million
Tagalog: 1.3 million
Vietnamese: 1.1 million
Korean: 967,000
Hmong: 200,000
Hawaiian: 27,160

sent to prison. Okada's book describes a Japanese American man's experiences after prison.

In 1976 Maxine Hong Kingston wrote *The Woman Warrior*. This memoir tells of her experience growing up as a Chinese American. She later wrote *China Men* (1980), which describes the lives of Chinese immigrants in Hawaii and North America. Hong Kingston was one of the first Asian American authors to gain widespread attention.

Amy Tan is a Chinese American from San Francisco, California. In 1989 she wrote a best-selling book about Asian American culture. This book, *The Joy Luck Club*, tells the story of a group of Chinese American women and their daughters. It talks about the struggles of holding on to Chinese traditions while growing up in the United States. In 1993

April 24, 1989

From the Pages of USA TODAY

For Amy Tan, it all began at college

Amy Tan remembers as a teen, she was so ashamed of her Shanghai-born mother she would walk several steps ahead so people wouldn't think they were together.

Those feelings—and a mother's reaction—are reflected in her best-selling first novel about the tensions and love between Chinese mothers and their U.S.-born daughters.

In *The Joy Luck Club*, a woman laments: "I am ashamed she is ashamed. Because she is my daughter and I am proud of her, and I am her mother but she is not proud of me."

Amy Tan no longer is ashamed, and her mother, Daisy, couldn't be prouder of her. "I'm glad to have such a daughter," says Daisy Tan, 72. "All the time she is so smart. Her writing is so smooth. And the stories are so good."

Amy Tan's best-selling book, *The Joy Luck Club*, talks about what it was like for Tan *(above)* to grow up as a Chinese American.

Critics and book-buyers agree. *The Joy Luck Club* (Putnam, $18.95) is No. 4 on the *New York Times* best-seller list. Vintage Books paid $1.2 million plus—

Hollywood producers turned *The Joy Luck Club* into a movie. Tan has written many more best-selling books, including *The Kitchen God's Wife*, *The Hundred Secret Senses*, and *Saving Fish from Drowning*.

Amy Tan paved the way for other Asian American writers. In 1991

beating eight others—for paperback rights.

"I can't think of another first novel in recent memory that has gone for that kind of money," says Vintage editor in chief Marty Asher. "It got the most extraordinary reviews of any novel, certainly any first novel, this year, and the love and enthusiasm it has generated is quite unprecedented."

Says a gratified Amy Tan, "Mothers have said to me the stories expressed a lot of things they haven't been able to express to their own daughters. They saw both sides of it—anger, extreme, deep love and everything in between."

Daisy Tan emigrated from Shanghai in 1949, escaping an abusive marriage that still gives her nightmares.

Once in northern California, she married Tan's father, a Beijing-educated electrical engineer who gave up an M.I.T. [Massachusetts Institute of Technoloy] scholarship to become a Baptist minister.

Their Oakland-born daughter remembers shunning her roots as a child, even crimping her nose with a clothespin to make it look less Chinese.

But Tan's real rebellion came in her teen years, after her father and brother died of brain tumors within months of each other. Daisy Tan took every last nickel they had to move the family from their "diseased house" to Europe.

There were few Asians in Switzerland and Amy was an exotic, sought-after date.

"I didn't feel as much ashamed of how I looked. I took up with some unseemly characters, started smoking, wearing eye makeup, shortening my skirts 5 inches [13 centimeters]."

Mother and daughter, living a subway ride away from each other in northern California, can laugh about that now. Their trip to China, which Tan vowed they would take after heart problems sent her mother to the hospital in 1986, erased any lingering conflicts the writer had about her Chinese-American identity.

Tan delved even deeper into her relationship with her mother and her dual heritage while writing the book. "I tried to speak more Chinese to her. She'd always had to speak to me in broken English; now it was up to me to speak in my fractured Chinese."

Since the book's publication, they've become even closer.

Recalls Amy Tan: "She was talking to me about something, going into a long explanation before she stopped and said, 'Oh, I don't need to tell you; you understand.' It was a great feeling, that she didn't have to explain it."

—*Tracey Wong Briggs*

Gus Lee published the acclaimed *China Boy*. In this memoir, Lee tells about growing up Chinese in San Francisco. Korean American Min Jin Lee wrote *Free Food for Millionaires* (2007). It is the story of a Korean immigrant family.

Jhumpa Lahiri is an Asian Indian American. In 2000 she won a Pulitzer Prize for *Interpreter of Maladies*, a short-story collection. She followed up with a novel called *The Namesake* (2003), which later became a movie. In these two works, Lahiri's characters are recent immigrants who struggle to be part of two different cultures. In 2008 Lahiri wrote *Unaccustomed Earth*. This short-story collection tells how different generations of Asian Indian Americans blend into U.S. culture.

Jhumpa Lahiri writes about the struggle of Asian Indian immigrants in the United States.

In 2008 Kao Kalia Yang published *The Latehomecomer: A Hmong Family Memoir*. The Hmong are a minority group in Laos, China, Vietnam, and Thailand. After the Vietnam War, many Hmong people fled Vietnam. They lived in refugee camps in Thailand and then moved to the United States. Yang's book tells of her family's escape from Vietnam, their experiences in a Thai camp, and their life in Minnesota.

Andrew X. Pham is from Ho Chi Minh City (formerly called

Kao Kalia Yang's Hmong family fled to the United States from Vietnam.

Saigon), Vietnam. He was born in 1967, at the height of the Vietnam War. In 1977 he and his family moved to California. In 1999 Pham published a book about his life called *Catfish and Mandala*. In *The Eaves of Heaven: A Life in Three Wars* (2008), he tells the story of his father's life in Vietnam and in the United States.

READ ALL ABOUT IT!

Many Asian Americans like to keep up with news from their home countries. They read newspapers, magazines, and websites written specifically for Asian Americans. Some newspapers are written in Asian languages. For instance, *Sing Tao Daily* is written in Chinese. *Korea Daily* is written in Korean. Other Asian American newspapers are written in English. The magazines *Thirteen Minutes* and *Jade* are English-language publications geared toward Asian Americans.

When walking through Chinatown or Koreatown in a big U.S. city, it is not uncommon to see signs printed in Asian languages. In some cities, you can hear Asian languages spoken on the radio. A television station in San Francisco broadcasts shows in Chinese. In Washington, D.C., a station features Vietnamese shows.

CHAPTER 2:

ARTS, MUSIC, AND MOVIES, MOVIES, MOVIES

In early Hollywood films, Asian American actors were usually cast in minor roles. The typical character was usually a "dragon lady" (a mean-spirited woman), a villain, or a faithful servant. One of the only Asian American movie heroes was the fictional Charlie Chan, a Chinese American detective. But a Chinese American actor did not get to play this leading part. European Americans made up to look Asian played the role in a series of Charlie Chan films made in the 1930s and 1940s.

Since the mid-twentieth century, opportunities for Asian American actors have improved. Asian Americans have starred in hundreds of feature films. Many of these movies deal with the Asian American experience.

The Joy Luck Club movie of 1993 tells the story of Chinese American mothers and daughters.

The 1993 movie version of *The Joy Luck Club* was based on Amy Tan's best-selling novel of the same name. The leading characters were played by Asian American women. They included Kieu

Chinh (Vietnamese American), Lisa Lu (Chinese American), Ming-Na (Chinese American), Tamlyn Tomita (Japanese and Filipino American), Lauren Tom (Chinese American), and Rosalind Chao (Chinese American). Wayne Wang directed the film. He was born in Hong Kong, a part of China.

Hawaiian-born Kayo Hatta is Japanese American. She wrote and directed a film called *Picture Bride* (1994). The movie takes place in the early 1900s. It tells the story of a Japanese woman who moves to Hawaii to marry a man she has never met. She and her future husband have seen each other only in photographs. "Picture brides" were common in the 1800s and early 1900s among Japanese and Koreans in the United States. The film won an Audience Award at the Sundance Film Festival in 1995.

Anna May Wong

Anna May Wong *(right)*, a Chinese American actress, acted in movies and on television. She worked from 1919 until her death in 1961. Her first films were silent pictures, or movies without sound.

Wong started acting at a time when Asian Americans suffered great discrimination. Asian American actors were offered only a few kinds of roles. Wong usually played a meek Chinese woman or a "dragon lady." Despite her limited roles, Wong rose to stardom. She was the first Asian American actress to become world famous.

This scene is from the 1999 film *Snow Falling on Cedars.* The film starred Japanese American actor Youki Kudoh *(left)* and Ethan Hawke *(right)*.

Snow Falling on Cedars (1999) tells the story of discrimination against Japanese Americans after World War II. The movie is based on a book of the same name. The movie stars Japanese American actress Youki Kudoh (who also appeared in *Picture Bride*) and Korean American actor Rick Yune.

In 2000 Filipino American director Gene Cajayon released *The Debut.* A debut is a large party that Filipino parents throw for their daughters when they turn eighteen. The film covers a conflict faced by many Asian immigrants. The parents want their children to follow the traditions of their home country, but the children want to become Americanized. *The Debut* stars Filipino American actor Dante Basco.

In 2006 Vietnamese American director Ham Tran released *Journey from the Fall.* All the money to produce the film came from

Vietnamese Americans. The movie tells the story of a Vietnamese family's struggle to survive after the Vietnam War. The story takes place in Vietnam and in California, where the family eventually moves.

In 2008, after twenty-three years of filming, directors Ellen Kuras and Thavisouk Phrasavath released *The Betrayal*. This documentary film tells the story of Phrasavath's family, Laotian refugees who immigrated to New York. The film was nominated in 2009 for an Academy Award for Best Documentary Feature Film.

Also in 2008, actor and director Clint Eastwood released *Gran Torino*. The movie stars Eastwood and Bee Vang. Vang is a Hmong American actor. The film is about a U.S. veteran of the Korean War (1950–1953) and his Hmong neighbors. It features a mostly Hmong American cast.

MARTIAL ARTS FILMS

Martial arts are traditional fighting arts. Asian martial arts include karate and kung fu. Since Ancient times, Asian soldiers have learned martial arts for use in warfare. In modern times, people learn martial arts for exercise, competitions, and self-defense. Many martial artists hone their skills by competing with other artists.

Asian martial arts involve dramatic, athletic movements, so martial arts can be exciting to watch. In the 1920s, filmmakers in China began making martial arts movies with lots of fight scenes. Over the years, many Asian martial arts movies were shown in the United States with English subtitles.

Enter the Dragon (1973) was made by a U.S. movie studio and a Hong Kong studio. The film was very successful and led to greater fame for its star, Chinese American Bruce Lee. Lee died shortly before the film was released.

Bruce Lee

Bruce Lee was born in San Francisco in 1940. His parents were Chinese Americans. When Lee was a boy, his family moved to Hong Kong. There Lee was a child film star. He also learned martial arts. He later returned to the United States, where he played many supporting roles in Hollywood films.

Bruce Lee captivated audiences around the world in the martial arts film *Enter the Dragon.*

Lee returned to Hong Kong to star in martial arts movies. *Fists of Fury* came out in 1971, and *Enter the Dragon* appeared in 1973. The films were produced jointly by U.S. and Hong Kong film studios. They became international hits. After the films came out, U.S. interest in martial arts skyrocketed. Lee died in 1973 of cerebral edema, or excess fluid in the brain. Worldwide, Bruce Lee is remembered as one of the best martial artists on film.

In the following decades, Hong Kong–born Jackie Chan and Jet Li became top martial arts movie stars. Chan, a director and actor, often combines martial arts and comedy. His films include *Rush Hour* (1998), *Rush Hour 2* (2001), *Shanghai Noon* (2000), and *Shanghai Knights* (2003). Jet Li has appeared in dozens of martial arts and action films in both China and the United States.

The film *Crouching Tiger, Hidden Dragon* (2000), directed by Ang Lee, was a huge success in the United States and around the world. This Chinese-language martial arts film tells the story of a stolen sword.

ASIANS BEHIND THE SCENES

Many Asian Americans work in the movie business behind the camera. They work as directors, producers, screenwriters, and set designers. Some Asian American filmmakers make Asian-themed movies. But many make movies that have nothing to do with their Asian heritage.

Director Ang Lee was born in Taiwan. In 1978 he moved to the United States. He studied theater and film production at the University of Illinois and at New York University. Lee's *Crouching Tiger, Hidden Dragon* is set in China. The movie features Chinese actors. But Lee has

Crouching Tiger, Hidden Dragon

Ang Lee's *Crouching Tiger, Hidden Dragon* received ten Academy Award nominations, more than any other Asian film. It won four Academy Awards, including Best Foreign Language Film. Several production companies from China, Hong Kong, Taiwan, and the United States worked together to create the movie.

Crouching Tiger, Hidden Dragon was released in 2000 to critical acclaim. It went on to win four Academy Awards.

Chinese actors speak Chinese throughout the film. During showings in the United States and other English-speaking countries, English subtitles appear across the bottom of the screen. Lee wanted the actors to speak Chinese instead of English because martial arts movies are part of Chinese culture. Lee explained, "Making a martial arts film in English to me is the same as John Wayne [a U.S. actor famous for playing rugged westerners] speaking Chinese in a Western."

also directed many movies with non-Asian actors. These include *Sense and Sensibility* (1995), *The Ice Storm* (1997), and *Brokeback Mountain* (2005) for which Lee won an Academy Award for best director.

Director and screenwriter M. Night Shyamalan is known for his suspenseful films.

M. Night Shyamalan was born in India and raised in the United States. He is a director and screenwriter. His best-known films are *The Sixth Sense* (1999), *Signs* (2002), *The Happening* (2008), and *The Last Airbender* (2010). Shyamalan's movies usually focus on the supernatural. They often have surprise endings. His films have received a total of seven Academy Award nominations.

Dean Devlin is a Filipino American producer and screenwriter. His films include *Independence Day* (1996), *Godzilla* (1998), *The Patriot* (2000), and *Flyboys* (2006). Hong Kong–born Wayne Wang directed *The Joy Luck Club* (1993), *Anywhere but Here* (1999), *Maid in Manhattan* (2002), and *Last Holiday* (2006).

Japanese American director Karyn Kusama

Director Karyn Kusama speaks at a press conference in 2009 in Toronto, Ontario. Her latest film is *Jennifer's Body*, released in 2009.

directed *Girlfight* (2000). This independent film tells the story of a Hispanic girl who takes up boxing. The film won awards at that year's Sundance Film Festival and the Cannes Film Festival.

MAKING MUSIC

Asian Americans are prominent in the world of classical music. In leading U.S. music schools, such as Juilliard in New York City, many students are Asian or Asian American. Many U.S. orchestras and classical ensembles feature Asian American musicians.

Cellist Yo-Yo Ma is one of the most famous musicians in the world. Ma was born in Paris, France, to Chinese parents. He began studying cello at the age of four. The family moved to the United States when Ma was seven. In his long career, Ma has performed solo and with chamber groups and orchestras. He has produced more than seventy-five albums and won fifteen Grammy Awards for musical excellence.

Classical musician Yo-Yo Ma is famous throughout the world for his cello playing. Here he performs at the Kodak Theatre in Hollywood, California, during the Academy Awards in 2005.

BLENDING MUSICAL TRADITIONS

Many Asian immigrants bring their musical instruments and musical traditions with them to the United States. With a group of fellow musicians, Cambodian American Sam-Ang Sam has released several albums of classical Khmer music. This music was played for Cambodian kings in earlier centuries. It features traditional instruments such as gongs, clappers, and drums. The Royal Laos Orchestra in Knoxville, Tennessee, is a group of Laotian American musicians. When they lived in Laos, they played music for the king.

Over the years, some Asian Americans have blended Asian folk music with American sounds. Chinese American Jon Jang creates symphonies based on Chinese folk music. Fred Ho, another Chinese American, blends traditional Asian music with African American jazz.

POP MUSIC

Several Asian Americans have found fame in pop and rock music. These stars include James Iha, former guitarist for the rock band Smashing Pumpkins. Iha is Japanese American. Singer-songwriter Norah Jones performs an eclectic mix of jazz, blues, pop, and soul music. She is of mixed

Norah Jones inherited talent from her father, musician Ravi Shankar, and from her mother, dancer Sue Jones.

Asian Indian and European descent. Allan Pineda Lindo, who goes by the stage name apl.de.ap, is in the hip-hop/pop group Black Eyed Peas. He is of Filipino American and African American descent. Mike Shinoda of the rock band Linkin Park is Japanese American and Russian American.

Birdie is the stage name of pop singer Souphak Xaphakdy. She sings about her experiences growing up as a Laotian American in Minnesota. At first, Birdie performed in her native Laotian. In 2007 she released her first album with all-English lyrics.

GRAPHIC ARTS

Japanese and Japanese Americans introduced manga, or Japanese comics, to the United States. The stories deal with many subjects, including romance, action, sports, fantasy, and mystery. The drawn characters usually have large, oval-shaped eyes and lots of hair. English editions of Japanese manga have been popular in the United States since the mid-1990s. Manga created in the United States is sometimes called Amerimanga or global manga.

Manga comics came from Japan to the United States in the late twentieth century.

A Real American Hero

Japanese American Larry Hama *(left)* is a famous comic-book writer. Hama created the series G. I. Joe: A Real American Hero. The storyline features a team of elite military spies code-named G. I. Joe. They fight members of Cobra, an evil terrorist organization. G. I. Joe comics have been around since 1942, but Hama introduced the G. I. Joe team. Marvel Comics published 155 issues of the series from 1982 to 1994. Larry Hama wrote almost every issue.

Much of the series' success was because of the strong characters. Hama served in the Vietnam War as an explosives expert. He based some of his characters on people he knew during the war. He based others on famous people in history. Some characters are martial artists, explosives experts, and ninjas (ancient Japanese fighters). Hama's female characters are all strong and independent. These characters have encouraged girls and women to read the series.

Hama worked to humanize all his characters, good and bad. "I came at [G.I. Joe] with an anti-war approach," he explains. "It's not that bad guys want to be bad. I wanted to peel away that mask and show their motivations. I wanted to develop characters that I thought were good, honorable, who followed a code of ethics. Villains are loyal, too."

Many cartoons, toys, and video games are based on the comic-book series that Hama wrote. In 2009 Hollywood released *G.I. Joe: The Rise of Cobra.* Japanese American Gerald Okamura and Chinese American Brandon Soo Hoo play leading roles in the film.

Anime is Japanese-style animation. The characters are hand-drawn or computer-generated. Anime television series, movies, and computer games are sometimes taken directly from manga. *Sailor Moon* and *Pokéman* are examples.

BUILDINGS AND MONUMENTS

A number of Asian Americans are famous architects. Maya Lin is a Chinese American architect from Ohio. She designed the Vietnam Veterans Memorial in Washington, D.C. This monument lists the names of U.S. service people killed during the Vietnam War. Each year

In 1985 Chinese American architect Maya Lin poses beside the famous memorial she designed—the Vietnam Veterans Memorial in Washington, D.C. People visit the memorial to honor those Americans killed in the Vietnam War.

January 18, 2007

From the Pages of USA TODAY

ImaginAsian tries to capture imagination of many groups

When Michael Hong, the 38-year-old CEO of ImaginAsian Entertainment, was a Korean-American kid growing up [in New York], he'd catch Asian martial-arts films in Manhattan theaters.

Twenty-five years later, media images of Asians have evolved from Bruce Lee to Jet Li. Hong hopes to further broaden the media landscape for Asians through ImaginAsian, a multimedia start-up that could be about to hit the big time. . . . ImaginAsian is [targeting] a growing U.S. audience of all ethnicities who like Asian-themed films and home videos, cable TV shows, music and Internet content.

Among ImaginAsian's more popular offerings: Japanese anime cartoons such as *Hikaru No Go*; Korean-produced soap operas; Bollywood movies from India's prolific film industry; Asian cooking, health and fitness shows; and original shows, including *Uncle Morty's Dub Shack*, a sitcom featuring the exploits of funky Asian-American rappers.

ImaginAsian is tapping into the growing mainstream interest in recent years in things Asian, from the popular Iron Chef cooking show to action films and dramas such as *Crouching Tiger, Hidden Dragon* and *Memoirs of a Geisha*.

Corporations covet the emerging crossover market of Asian-American, immigrant and white consumers—from their teens to their 30s—who are embracing the globalization of the media, products and technology.

more than three million people visit the memorial, which opened in 1982. Lin also designed the Museum of Chinese in America. It opened in New York City in 2009.

I. M. Pei is a world-famous Chinese American architect. He is

Henry Jenkins, co-director of MIT's Comparative Media Studies program and author of *Convergence Culture: Where Old and New Media Collide*, calls it "pop cosmopolitanism."

"At one time, the wisdom was that Asian content needed to be westernized to appeal to the West," Jenkins writes in an e-mail interview.

"But now, kids are seeking out the most Asian of content because it does not look and feel like American-made media."

Corporate advertisers used to ignore the small numbers of Asian-American consumers, says CEO Bill Imada of the IW Group, a marketing firm in Los Angeles.

But today, businesses the world over are aiming at that demographic group.

"There's critical mass now," Imada says.

Phil Yu, a 28-year-old film school graduate of the University of Southern California and author of a blog on Asian-American media issues (www.AngryAsianMan.com), says ImaginAsian offers films and TV shows that reflect his life as a young Korean-American. "It's good to see programming that represents us, and not only the white mainstream pop culture," Yu says.

While ImaginAsian's early fans were mostly Asian-American, today more than 60% of its audience is white and other ethnicities, executives say.

[Michael] Hong says. "We want to be accessible to all Asians and non-Asians."

To that end, ImaginAsian offers IATV, a 24-hour national network devoted to Asian-American topics; the ImaginAsian movie theater in New York; ImaginAsian Radio, a weekly radio show featuring Asian-American music and news; and IALink, a website for Asian issues.

This year and next, ImaginAsian will release 25 feature films and home videos, including *Journey from the Fall*, an acclaimed drama by young filmmaker Ham Tran about the fate of a Vietnamese family after the fall of Saigon.

"Asian-Americans are an unbelievably dynamic demographic," [AZT Television vice president Bill] Georges says. "They deserve content targeted to them."

—Edward Iwata

known for his modern, high-tech designs. He designed the Javits Convention Center in New York City; the Rock and Roll Hall of Fame in Cleveland, Ohio; the famous glass pyramid at the Louvre museum in Paris, France; among other creations.

CHAPTER 3:
PLAY BALL!

From the martial arts to the Olympics, sports have long been an important part of Asian culture. Most popular U.S. sports, such as baseball, basketball, soccer, ice hockey, and golf, are also popular in Asia. In the early twentieth century, discrimination kept most Asian Americans off professional playing fields in the United States. But since the late 1900s, more and more Asian Americans have been joining professional U.S. teams. Asian Americans have also represented the United States in the Olympic Games.

In addition to playing sports, Asian Americans participate as spectators. Like other Americans, they follow sports such as professional baseball and basketball in the United States. Some Asian immigrants also follow sports in their home countries. They root for Asian teams that play cricket, rugby, and other sports that are not widely played in the United States.

PROFESSIONAL ATHLETES

Walter Tin Kit Achiu was the first Asian American to play professional sports in the United States. From

OPPOSITE PAGE: Speed skater Apolo Anton Ohno competes during the 2010 Winter Olympics in Vancouver, British Columbia.

THIS PAGE: Asian American fans of the Philadelphia Eagles cheer on their football team at a game in November 2009.

Dat Nguyen *(pictured on right)* was the first Vietnamese American to play in the NFL. Here he celebrates with a Dallas Cowboys teammate after a victory.

1927 to 1928, he played football for the Dayton (Ohio) Triangles. Achiu was a Chinese American from Hawaii. After his football career, he became a professional wrestler. Al Lolotai was also from Hawaii. His family was originally from Samoa, a chain of Pacific Islands. Lolotai played for the Washington Redskins of the National Football League (NFL) in 1945 and the Los Angeles Dons of the All-America Football Conference from 1946 to 1949.

In modern times, Asian Americans are more common in the NFL. From 1992 to 1997, Korean American Eugene Chung played as an offensive linebacker for the New England Patriots, the Jacksonville Jaguars, and the Indianapolis Colts. Dat Nguyen, the son of immigrants, was the first Vietnamese American to play in the NFL. He played linebacker for the Dallas Cowboys from 2001 to 2006.

Baseball is popular in Asia and among Asian Americans. In 1964 Masanori Murakami was the first Japanese player in the U.S. major leagues. He pitched for the San Francisco Giants for one year before heading back to Japan. Hideo Nomo,

Hideo Nomo pitches for the Los Angeles Dodgers in a 1995 game against the Pittsburgh Pirates.

Baseball Crazy

Wally Yonamine *(right)* was born to Japanese immigrants in Hawaii in 1925. He became the first Japanese American to play professional football when he signed with the San Francisco 49ers in 1947. When an injury forced him to stop playing football, he turned to baseball. In 1951 a Japanese team called the Tokyo Yomiuri Giants recruited Yonamine. He played U.S.-style baseball, which was much rougher than the Japanese game. He stole bases aggressively and slid into home plate. At first the Japanese crowds booed him and threw rocks at him. But he was such a successful player that the Japanese adopted his U.S. style of play.

another recruit from Japan, played on eight different U.S. major-league teams. He retired in 2008. Nomo's success on the field opened the door for many other Asian Americans in baseball.

Benny Agbayani was born in Honolulu, Hawaii. He is of Filipino and Samoan descent. Beginning in 1998, he played baseball with the New York Mets, the Colorado Rockies, and the Boston Red Sox. Other Asian American baseball players include Ron Darling (Chinese American), Danny Graves (Vietnamese American), Jim Parque (Vietnamese American), and Lenn Sakata (Japanese American).

In 1946 Wat Misaka, a Japanese American from Utah, became the first nonwhite to play professional basketball. That year, he was the New York Knicks' number one draft pick. At 7 feet 6 inches (228

Chinese basketball star Yao Ming has gained fame throughout the United States since he entered the NBA in 2001 as a Houston Rocket.

cm), basketball player Yao Ming is the tallest player in the National Basketball Association. Ming was born in China, where he played for the Chinese Basketball Association. He plays for the Houston Rockets.

Michelle Wie, a Korean American, started playing golf at the age of four. "The first time I grabbed a golf club, I knew that I'd do it for the rest of my life," she says.

She turned professional in 2005, at the age of sixteen. Wie is a regular on the Ladies Professional Golf Association (LPGA) Tour. In November 2009, Wie won her first LPGA Tour title with a victory at the Lorena Ochoa Invitational golf tournament in Mexico.

Richard Park is one of the few Asian Americans playing professional hockey. A Korean American, Park has played for the Pittsburgh Penguins, the Minnesota Wild, and the Vancouver Canucks. In 2006 he signed with the New York Islanders.

Korean American golfer Michelle Wie swings her club at the Dubai Ladies Masters in 2009, where she finished in second place.

Figure skater Michelle Kwan earned a silver medal in the 1998 Olympics and a bronze in the 2002 Olympics.

OLYMPIANS

Several Asian Americans have shone at the Olympic Games. Kristi Yamaguchi is a Japanese American from California. Yamaguchi started ice skating at a young age to help correct a birth defect called club feet. She soon became a champion. In 1992 she won the Olympic gold medal in women's figure skating. Chinese American figure skater Michelle Kwan is another Olympic medalist. Speed skater Apolo Anton Ohno has won eight Olympic medals, which makes him the most decorated U.S. Winter Olympian. He earned medals at the 2002, 2006, and 2010 Winter Olympics. He is the son of a European American mother and a Japanese American father.

Amy Chow is a Chinese American gymnast. In 1996 she and six other Americans took the Olympic gold medal in the women's gymnastics team competition. The talented team became known as the Magnificent Seven. Chow was the first Asian American to win the gold medal in gymnastics.

U.S. Olympic Firsts

Asian American Olympic history goes back to 1948. That year, Sammy Lee and Victoria Manalo-Draves became the first Asian Americans to win gold medals. Both athletes were divers. Sammy Lee, the son of Korean immigrants, won a gold medal in platform diving and a bronze medal for the springboard. Manalo-Draves was the daughter of an English-immigrant mom and a Filipino-immigrant dad. She won gold medals in both platform diving and springboard

Divers Sammy Lee *(left)* and Victoria Manalo-Draves *(right)* faced discrimination at home in the United States but triumphed at the 1948 Olympics in London, England.

While training for the Olympics, both divers faced discrimination. Lee trained in Pasadena, California. In that city, African Americans, Asians, and other people of color could use the city pool only once a week. Afterward, city workers drained the pool and refilled it so that white swimmers did not share water with people of color. For a time, Manalo-Draves's coach had Victoria use her mother's maiden name, Taylor. This name sounded more "American" than Manalo. The coach thought it would make her more acceptable to U.S. fans. Manolo-Draves was also separated from white divers when she trained for the Olympics.

Tiffany Roberts is a Filipino American soccer player. From 1994 to 1999, she played with the U.S. Women's National Team. She was part of the first-ever gold-medal-winning women's soccer team at the Olympic Games in 1996.

FROM ASIA TO AMERICA

A number of sports that originated in Asia have become U.S. favorites. Surfing has been a popular sport in Hawaii for centuries. Hawaiians and other Pacific Islanders first surfed on their bellies. Early Hawaiians were probably the first people to stand up on the boards to surf.

Hawaiian Duke Kahanamoku, pictured here in 1938, helped bring surfing from Hawaii to the mainland United States.

Duke Kahanamoku, a native Hawaiian, is called the Father of Modern Surfing. In 1912 and 1920, he won gold medals as an Olympic swimmer. At that time, surfing was popular only in the Pacific Islands. Kahanamoku used his Olympic fame to introduce the sport to the rest of the world. In the twenty-first century, millions of Americans have taken up the sport.

Martial arts have also traveled from Asia to America. Asian martial arts emerged in about 480 B.C. in China and India. Since then, all Asian countries have developed unique forms of martial arts. Americans started to learn about martial arts during World War II and the Korean War (1950–1953).

A tae kwon do master instructs a young student in this form of martial arts, which originated in Korea.

June 11, 2002

From the Pages of USA TODAY

Korean-Americans unite for game; In L.A., fans cheer for home country

They tied the Korean flag around their necks as if it were a cape, wore Red Devil T-shirts to symbolize their country, joined in Korean chants and celebrated wildly when Ahn Jung-hwan scored his team's lone goal.

It didn't matter that many of the 350 Koreans gathered at Rosen Brewery to watch South Korea and the United States tie 1-1 in World Cup competition couldn't name the players.

"I'm not much of a soccer fan. But when the World Cup rolls around and you know that your home country Korea is in the World Cup, it's something that you become a fan of just because of that," said Kyu Lee, 23. He wore a No. 25 jersey his cousin had made for him during his visit to South Korea last week. Like many others here, he was born in Korea but is an American citizen. "It's a world event, and it's important to root for where you come from."

Rosen, located in Koreatown, just west of downtown and southeast of Hollywood, was just one of the many places Koreans gathered to watch the game in the city.

They arrived as early as 4 p.m. PT [Pacific time] to get a seat, taking in the Los Angeles Lakers-New Jersey Nets game beforehand, in front of the 180-inch [457 cm] screen where they watched on KTE, a Korean station.

Francis Hur, executive director of the Korean American Federation, which put together the event, is a soccer fan. But he said this was about more than the match. "Most [Koreans] who were born here realize their identification after going to the colleges. This kind of event makes them realize it. It's a big chance to understand what Korea is."

The 11:30 p.m. local time start didn't deter fans, as it was standing room only with about 100 turned away.

The Kims, Byron, 38, and Seonmi, 30, brought their 6-year-old son, Howard, whose face was painted in red, blue and black. "He wants this," Byron said of his son's desire to watch the game. By halftime, little Howard was fast asleep, able to block out the screaming, chanting and occasional drum pounding.

Not every Korean cheered for their country. Recent University California-Davis grad Andy Suh, 21, speculated that if the USA won perhaps it would bring more attention to the sport. "This is the biggest sporting event in the world," Suh said. "Besides getting attention on ESPN, you don't see that much World Cup coverage. I think it would be really good for the sport if U.S. wins."

Palmdale [California] resident Rick Case, 44, was among the handful of Americans with the guts to venture inside a Korean bar. "I've got to go into the wolves' den," said Case, one of those arriving at 4 p.m. He was torn about which team to cheer for. "I was sort of pulling for Korea because I look at it like the USA could learn a little bit from the Korean culture," said Case, who was born and raised in nearby Venice. "I've got a lot of respect for the Korean people and culture."

—Kelly Carter

U.S. soldiers saw Korean, Indonesian, and Japanese soldiers using martial arts in combat. The U.S. military then trained some U.S. soldiers in martial arts. In the 1960s and 1970s, movies starring martial artists such as Bruce Lee made martial arts even more popular.

Ancient martial arts have evolved into many different types. Karate (Japanese), aikido (Japanese), kung fu (Chinese), tai chi (Chinese), and tae kwon do (Korean) are some of the most common forms of martial arts practiced in the United States. Asian Americans compete in these sports, but they are just as popular among non–Asian Americans.

CHAPTER 4:

EAST MEETS WEST

Asian immigrants to the United States bring their religious beliefs with them. Depending on their home countries, some Asian immigrants practice Buddhism, Hinduism, Islam, or another Eastern religion. Other Asian immigrants practice Christianity, the most common religion in the United States.

ASIA'S BIG THREE RELIGIONS

Buddhism is one of the most common religions in Asia. A teacher named Siddhartha Gautama, known as the Buddha, founded the practice in India in about 500 B.C. In modern times, the religion is widespread in Japan, Southeast Asia, Sri Lanka, and other parts of Asia. Buddhists believe in a cycle of life, death, and rebirth. By living a noble life, Buddhists hope to achieve a state of peace and happiness. Asian immigrants have brought Buddhism with them to the United States. They have established Buddhist temples, monasteries (religious communities), and schools in U.S. cities. The largest U.S. Buddhist temples are in

OPPOSITE PAGE: Americans of many backgrounds participate in a Buddhist meditation ceremony in Ojai, California.

THIS PAGE: A statue of the Buddha, the founder of Buddhism

Hindu priests honor the shrine of Krishna, a Hindu god. This Hindu temple is in Greenbelt, Maryland.

California. They include the Hsi Lai Temple in Hacienda Heights and the City of Ten Thousand Buddhas in Talmage.

Hinduism also started in India. Its roots are thousands of years old. In modern times, most Asian Indians are Hindus. Hindus also believe in a cycle of life, death, and rebirth. They believe that only those who achieve spiritual perfection move on to a higher state of existence. Asian Indians have brought Hinduism to the United States. Like Asian Buddhists, they have opened Hindu temples and religious centers in U.S. cities.

More Eastern Religions

Buddhism, Hinduism, and Islam are the major religions of Asia. But Asians practice other faiths too. These faiths include Confucianism and Taoism (practiced mostly in China), Shintoism (practiced in Japan), and Jainism and Sikhism (practiced in India).

A man named Muhammad founded the Islamic religion on the Arabian Peninsula in the A.D. 600s. Islam is common in the Middle East and North Africa. However, many Asian Indians and Southeast Asians also practice Islam. Many Asian immigrants practice Islam in the United States. People who practice Islam are called Muslims. Through prayer, study, and behavior, they strive for oneness with Allah, or God.

Bangladeshi American teens attend an Asian culture festival in Florida. Their head coverings are part of traditional Islamic dress.

A Korean American pastor stands near the Protestant church he leads in Wheeling, Illinois.

CHURCH AND COMMUNITY

Christianity is the most common religion in the United States. It is also practiced in parts of Asia. For instance, many people in Vietnam and the Philippines practice Catholicism, a major branch of Christianity. Many Koreans practice Protestantism, another major branch. Some immigrants from Asia bring their Christian practices with them to the United States. Others convert to Christianity in the United States.

Many U.S. Christian groups have assisted Asian immigrants. For instance, some U.S. Lutheran churches helped Vietnamese refugees settle in the United States after the Vietnam War.

Buddhist and Hindu temples, Islamic mosques (houses of worship), and Christian churches all serve as community centers for Asians in the United States. They offer not only places to practice religion but also a way for Asian immigrants to form bonds with one another.

December 27, 2002

From the Pages of USA TODAY

Postcards from the road; Zen monastery brings memories of the departed to light

"Going on means going far, going far means returning," the ancient Chinese philosopher and mystic Lao Tsu wrote.

Centuries later, during a visit to a Zen Buddhist monastery a few weeks after our mothers' deaths, my husband and I affirmed those words in ways we had never imagined.

Tucked into a thickly forested, improbably remote corner of the Catskills just three hours north of Manhattan [New York], the Japanese-style Dai Bosatsu Zendo draws students from across the globe for disciplined monastic training. But not all pilgrims [religious seekers] arrive with shaved heads, straight backs and the ability to think mindfully at 5 a.m.

Some, like us, come for o-bon, a summer Buddhist festival that honors the spirits of departed ancestors and friends.

Commemorated throughout Japan, o-bon reunites the living and the dead through such traditional rituals as bonfires, graveyard visits and the placement of favorite foods and photographs on family altars.

We arrived at the monastery late on a Saturday afternoon, hoping to shed some of our accumulated stress with the shoes we dutifully placed on the stone entryway.

We weren't disappointed. After dropping our bags in an ascetically furnished room overlooking Lake Beecher and pausing at an o-bon altar dedicated to the victims of Sept. 11, we joined several other participants at a low wooden table. Wielding long, thin brushes and pots of black ink, we wrote our mothers' names on diaphanous paper lanterns before reclaiming our shoes for a serene amble along a sun-dappled path.

The next time we saw our lanterns, they had been transformed.

Now aglow with candles, they glimmered in the growing darkness like celestial fireflies. But as we discovered, their final journey would be by water rather than air.

Following the abbott's lead, we filed silently to the edge of Beecher Lake. Placing our lanterns on one of two boats, we watched as rowers headed to the far shore and set them adrift one by one.

According to o-bon legend, floating lanterns carry the spirits of loved ones safely back to the other world. And that night, as they bobbled on a mirrored surface so smooth we could almost see the reflected smudge of the Perseids meteor shower above us, I became a believer.

—Laura Bly

Above: A Hindu couple in traditional clothing pose on the Golden Gate Bridge in San Francisco, California. *Left:* These two women wear traditional Indian dress and red marks called *bindis* between their eyebrows.

BETWEEN TWO WORLDS

Clothing can be an important part of religious practice. Some Asian religions require a person to wear a certain kind of clothing, headdress, or other marking. For instance, the Sikh religion of India traditionally requires its followers to leave their hair uncut and to cover it with a turban. Many Hindus also wear turbans. Many Muslim women wear the hijab. This head covering is meant to conceal a woman's beauty from men other than her husband. Wearing the hijab is an expression of modesty for Muslim women. Some married Hindi women wear a bindi, a red mark between their eyebrows. The bindi symbolizes female energy, which is said to be strongest on the forehead. The mark is meant to protect a married couple from evil spirits.

In many parts of Asia, such religious dress is commonplace. But in the United States, people wearing turbans, hijabs, and other religious clothing sometimes stand out. Some Americans are fearful of people who dress differently. They sometimes insult and discriminate against people wearing Eastern religious dress. Some of the worst hostility occurred after the September 11, 2001, terrorist attacks in the United States. Muslim terrorists carried out the attacks. They caused the deaths of about three thousand people in New York City; Arlington, Virginia; and rural Pennsylvania. After the attacks, some Americans lashed out at people they thought were Muslims. Some people confused Muslims and Hindus. They attacked Hindu temples and men wearing turbans.

Because of such treatment, some Asian immigrants give up their religious dress in the United States. They want to fit into U.S. society. Young Asian immigrants often feel caught between two worlds. Their parents want them to wear religious clothing. But they want to blend in with their classmates.

Not all Americans are suspicious of Asian religions. In fact, many non–Asian Americans have adopted Asian religious practices. For instance, many Americans practice yoga. Yoga is a mental and spiritual practice that developed in Hindu teaching. Other non—Asian Americans practice Buddhist meditation. Meditation is a spiritual practice designed to bring people to a state of peace and relaxation.

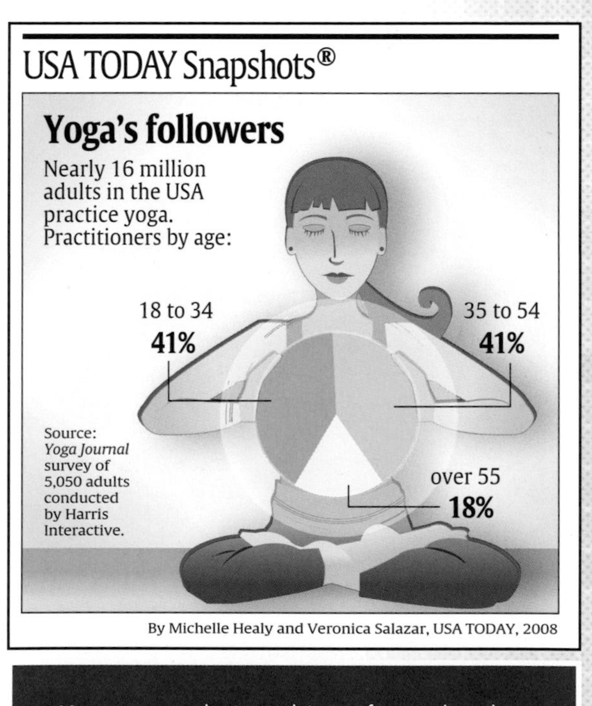

Yoga came to the United States from India. The Hindu practice offers many physical and spiritual benefits.

CHAPTER 5:
LET'S CELEBRATE!

Across the United States, Asian Americans celebrate holidays and festivals from their homelands. Some of these celebrations are huge, with colorful parades. Some of the rituals and practices are based on ancient traditions. Often, many non–Asian Americans join in the festivities.

NEW YEAR

The biggest nonreligious holiday for Asian Americans is the New Year. Some Asians call it the Lunar New Year. Others call it the Spring Festival. The Vietnamese name for New Year is Tet Nguyen Dan, or Tet for short. The name means "the first morning of the first day of the new period."

Participants walk in the Chinese New Year Parade in New York City's Chinatown. The Chinese New Year is the start of the year based on the lunar (moon) calendar.

By any name, New Year is a time to welcome and celebrate the new season and new beginnings. Asian New Year celebrations do not fall on the same day each year or even in the same month. Most occur

A Muslim woman commemorates Muharram in a religious procession in New York City.

in January or February. The dates depend on the cycle of the moon.

Muslim Asians observe New Year on the first day of Muharram. Muharram is the first month in the Islamic calendar. It falls at different times of the year, depending on the lunar calendar. In addition to ringing in the New Year, the holiday commemorates Muhammad's journey between two Arabian cities, Mecca and Medina. From Medina, Muhammad founded an Islamic empire. Some Asian American Muslims exchange greeting cards on this day. Most spend the day reflecting on the New Year to come.

The Chinese New Year is the best-known Asian American New Year celebration. The celebration begins in January or February, on the day of the first new moon of the year. It typically lasts until the first full moon of the year—about fifteen days.

Each Asian American group celebrates the New Year in its own way. But the different celebrations have much in common. In all Asian cultures, the New Year is a time to get rid of old, bad luck and to welcome new, good luck. It's also a time to spend with family and to respect elders and ancestors. Many Asian Americans clean their homes of all clutter and dust to honor the New Year. They pay debts and settle old arguments with family and friends. They also wear brand-new outfits. These activities are meant to shed negative energy and make room for positive energy.

RELIGIOUS HOLIDAYS

Many Asian Americans celebrate during religious holidays. Every fall, Hindus and followers of some other Asian religions celebrate Diwali Day. This holiday is also called the Festival of Lights. Each group ties the celebration to a different historical event. But in all cases, the festival celebrates the victory of good over evil. In some parts of India, Diwali Day is also a New Year's celebration.

These Asian Americans light candles to celebrate Diwali Day, or the Festival of Lights, in Queens, New York.

Among Hindus, the festival lasts for five days. Before the celebration, people clean their homes to make room for good luck. They decorate their homes with colorful paper lanterns and small clay lamps. Families sometimes light hundreds of lamps in their homes. They believe the Hindu goddess of good luck visits homes that are brightly lit. Being with family, eating sweets, setting off firecrackers, and exchanging presents are also part of Diwali celebrations. In the United States, cities with large Asian Indian populations hold fairs to celebrate Diwali Day. The Diwali Day celebration in Washington, D.C., attracts thousands of people each year.

Every year, Muslims, including Asian Muslims, observe the holy month of Ramadan. Ramadan is the ninth month of the Islamic calendar. It falls at a different time each year. During Ramadan, Muslims fast (do not eat) between sunrise and sunset. Through prayer and fasting, Muslims purify their bodies and souls. Ramadan ends with a three-day festival known as Eid al-Fitr. During this festival, families gather to eat, dance, and exchange gifts.

Christmas celebrates the birth of Jesus. He was an ancient Jewish teacher whose life provided the basis for Christianity. Christian Asian Americans celebrate Christmas by

Whether or not they are Christians, many Asian Americans celebrate with friends and family at Christmastime.

decorating trees, going to church, gathering with friends and family, and exchanging gifts. Many non-Christian Asian Americans celebrate Christmas too, because the holiday is such a big part of U.S. culture. Christmas is a day off for most Americans. Asian Americans take advantage of the time off to get together with family.

DOUBLE FIFTH

On the fifth day of the fifth month of the lunar calendar, Chinese people celebrate the Dragon Boat Festival. The day usually falls in late May or June. Because of the day it's held, the celebration is sometimes called Double Fifth. Celebrations occur in Chinese cities as well as in Chinese American communities in the United States.

Participants race a long, thin dragon boat as part of the Dragon Boat Festival, a traditional Chinese holiday. This race takes place in Olympia, Washington.

June 16, 1992

From the Pages of USA TODAY

U.S. teams take to "drag" racing

Two U.S. teams battled monsoon rains and choppy waters on the Kowloon waterfront Sunday but finished strong in the annual Hong Kong Dragon Boat Festival, an event revered among Asian cultures but practically unknown in the USA.

The U.S. Dragon Boat Association of Philadelphia, the reigning U.S. champion, finished third in the 20-boat men's division dominated by the Indonesian Rowing and Canoeing Association for the second consecutive year.

A San Diego team was fourth in a women's division dominated by the 700-member False Creek Women's Dragon Boat Team of Vancouver.

The art of 20 paddlers (10 pairs) moving their arms in synchronized motion is linked to a 2,000-year-old Chinese legend.

The boats, with a dragon head at the prow, are painted in traditional Chinese colors and teams adhere to certain rituals.

A drummer sits on a very unstable chair near the top of the prow and beats out a cadence with input from a steersman stationed at the back of the 40-foot [12-meter], 1,800-pound [816-kilogram] boats.

Crew weight and strategy affect maneuverability and speed. When necessary, crews have been known to downsize by having designated paddlers jump overboard.

With boats sprinting in six lanes of a 640-meter course, winners paddle between 70 to 100 strokes a minute and complete the course in less than three minutes.

The U.S. men stayed close. "We were only .03 seconds behind Shun De from China and only 1.7 seconds behind the Indonesians," said Dr. Dave Wald, one of four physicians on the Philadelphia team. "That's only a couple strokes."

—Elaine Davis

Many activities at this festival involve warding off disease and evil spirits. At noon, people try to make eggs stand on end. It is said that those who succeed will have good luck. Festivalgoers also race long, narrow canoes called dragon boats. The boats vary in size. Some boats can fit up to fifty paddlers. Some are adorned with dragon heads. The boat races are a colorful sight. Festival-goers also eat *zongzi* at the Dragon Boat Festival. These are balls of rice, meat, fruit, and vegetables wrapped in bamboo leaves.

Other Asian American groups also celebrate on the fifth day of the fifth month. Their festivals are similar to the Dragon Boat Festival but have some variations. For instance, Japanese Americans celebrate Kodomo No Hi, or Children's Day, on the fifth day of the fifth month. This celebration honors children and their happiness. People eat *chimaki*—a sweet rice paste wrapped in bamboo leaves. They hang one colorful fish-shaped flag for each child in the household. Korean Americans celebrate Dano on the fifth day of the fifth month. On this day, they wear red and blue to ward off disease.

The Vietnamese celebrate Tet Doan Ngo on the fifth day of the fifth month. The Vietnamese believe that yang, or male energy, is at its strongest at this time of year. So on this holiday, Vietnamese and Vietnamese Americans celebrate maleness. They also honor the summer solstice (the longest day of the year).

This young girl participates in a Children's Day, or Kodomo No Hi, celebration in Florida. Japanese Americans celebrate this day on the fifth day of the fifth month according to the lunar calendar.

Chinese Firecrackers

Americans watch fireworks displays on July 4 to celebrate U.S. independence. The Chinese invented fireworks in about 200 B.C. Historians think that someone threw green bamboo shoots into a fire to help keep the flames burning. The green shoots turned black. Then, unexpectedly, they exploded. The sound scared people and animals. The Chinese decided that the *pao chuk*, or "bursting bamboo," would also scare away evil spirits.

For the next one thousand years, the Chinese used pao chuk every New Year to frighten evil spirits. Eventually, people added gunpowder to the bamboo to create bigger and louder blasts. Beginning in the 1400s, Italian fireworks makers turned fireworks into an art form. Using chemicals, they made firecrackers that exploded into different shapes and colors. They shot fireworks into the air to light up the night sky.

The fascination with fireworks spread across Europe. When British settlers came to North America, they brought firecrackers with them. July 4 fireworks displays started in 1777, exactly one year after the signing of the Declaration of Independence. In the following centuries, fireworks makers again improved fireworks. They added new chemicals to add more colors to the explosions.

INDEPENDENCE DAYS

Asian Americans celebrate U.S. Independence Day on July 4, just as other Americans do. In addition, some Asian Americans celebrate their homeland's independence day. For instance, on August 14, Pakistani Americans celebrate Pakistan's Independence Day. Pakistani Americans in New York hold a big festival on this day.

Filipino American women take part in the Philippine Independence Day Parade in New York City.

In June Filipinos celebrate Philippine Independence Day. The yearly Philippine Independence Day Parade in New York is the largest gathering of Filipino Americans in the nation.

AMERICAN-BORN ASIAN CELEBRATIONS

In addition to celebrating holidays, Asian Americans hold parades and festivals simply to showcase their cultures. Filipinos hold the Pistahan Festival in San Francisco. At this celebration, festivalgoers promote Filipino American art and business. The National Cherry Blossom Festival

Chinese Thanksgiving

The Mid-Autumn Festival, or Moon Festival, is the Chinese thanksgiving. It takes place in fall, usually in September, on the day the moon is brightest. The Moon Festival celebrates a good harvest. At this festival, the Chinese send their wishes to the moon goddess and eat pastries called moon cakes.

In 1912 the Tokyo mayor donated cherry trees to the city of Washington, D.C., in an effort to recognize and enhance U.S.–Japanese friendship. In modern times, the springtime National Cherry Blossom Festival in Washington, D.C. *(above)*, celebrates Japanese culture.

in Washington, D.C., is a two-week spring celebration. It is a time to show off the city's blossoming cherry trees. In 1912 the city of Tokyo, Japan, gave the trees to Washington, D.C., to honor the friendship between Japan and the United States. The celebration includes Japanese music, dancing, food, crafts, and a parade.

In 1992 the U.S. government designated the month of May as Asian Pacific American Heritage Month. Throughout the United States, Asian Americans hold festivals, parades, and dances during this month. The celebrations honor Asian American achievements.

CHAPTER 6:

ASIAN FOODS

Asian immigrants to the United States have brought their cooking traditions with them. Some have opened restaurants. In this way, they have introduced Asian foods to other Americans. The Asian diet is one of the more healthful diets in the world. It features fresh vegetables, rice, and seafood. Chefs prepare many kinds of spices and sauces. The ingredients in Asian foods vary, depending on location.

THREE TYPES OF ASIAN COOKING

Southwest Asia includes India, Pakistan, Sri Lanka, Bangladesh, and Myanmar (also called Burma). This region has its own special style of cooking. The climate and soil of Southwest Asia are suited to growing wheat. People use the wheat to make flatbreads called naan and chapati. Cooks in this region use flavorful spices and sauces. Asian Indian cooks use a blend of spices called curry. Curry features turmeric, cloves, cumin, and hot peppers. Southwest Asians drink milk from

OPPOSITE PAGE: This plate of steamed vegetables and chicken is typical of Asian fare.

THIS PAGE: Curry is commonly used in Indian cuisine, such as this spicy potato curry dish.

goats and cows. They also use the milk to make butter, yogurt, and cheese. Ghee is an oil made by boiling down unsalted butter. It is used in many Indian dishes. Southwest Asia is home to many Hindus. To Hindus, cows are sacred. So Hindus do not eat beef.

Northeast Asia includes China, Korea, and Japan. Rice grows well in this region. It forms the basis for many meals. Noodles are another staple of Northeast Asian meals. People in Northeast Asia also eat stir-fried or grilled vegetables, fish, and tofu. They don't eat much red meat or dairy products. Some Northeast Asian food is very spicy. Japanese food is very distinctive. It includes tempura. This popular dish consists of vegetables or seafood dipped in batter and fried. Sushi is raw fish wrapped in rice and seaweed. Preparing sushi is an art form for Japanese chefs. They take great care to use the freshest fish. They work to make platters of sushi look very appealing.

Once eaten only in Japan, sushi has become a U.S. favorite.

Cucumber with Crab

This refreshing Japanese combination of cucumber slices and crabmeat has a tart dressing made with vinegar. You could use shrimp or scallops in place of crab. Or serve the cucumber and dressing alone.

INGREDIENTS

2 cucumbers, peeled and seeded
1 teaspoon salt
6 ounces (¾ cup) canned or frozen and thawed crab
sesame seeds (optional)

DRESSING

¼ cup rice vinegar
2 tablespoons sugar
¼ teaspoon soy sauce

PREPARATION

1. Thinly slice cucumbers, place in a bowl, and sprinkle with salt. Let stand for 5 minutes. Then use your hands to gently squeeze the water out of the cucumbers.
2. Break up crab into small pieces.
3. In another bowl, combine vinegar, sugar, and soy sauce.
4. Put cucumber and crabmeat in 4 small bowls and add dressing. Sprinkle with sesame seeds if desired.

Serves 4

February 22, 2008

From the Pages of USA TODAY

Pan-Asian fresh eateries; They're using the old noodle in bold, affordable new ways

Now that American diners have digested the rituals of the sushi bar, several more styles of casual Asian dining are poised to enter the mainstream and expand the comfort-food universe.

Modern (and often Westernized) noodle bars and pan-Asian small-plates eateries are beginning to pop up around the country. Some are branches of popular Asian eateries from Tokyo and London, while others are brands launched by American restaurant franchisers. Still others have won prestigious national culinary [cooking] honors and critical acclaim.

With America's Asian population growing and a wave of young food-savvy diners embracing low-priced casual dining and exotic flavors, the time may be right for an Asian renaissance.

"There is such a fervor for it, a whole culture behind it," says David Chang, chef/owner of Momofuku Noodle Bar and Momofuku Ssam Bar in New York. "People are appreciating it more, and they understand it's not just sushi."

[Asian food] received a major boost last year at the James Beard awards when the Korean-American Chang was named rising star chef and his Momofuku Ssam Bar was nominated for best new restaurant. Chang had built his reputation over the past four years with the tiny and sleek Noodle Bar, which serves bowls of ramen noodles in broth topped with high-quality organic ingredients.

In 2006, he opened the cafeteria-style Ssam Bar (ssam is Korean for "anything wrapped") to showcase dishes of meat and rice encased in flour pancakes. This spring, he plans to open Momofuku KO, a 14-seat restaurant also in New York that will serve creative "vaguely Asian" dishes, but "is really food without borders."

On a larger scale, two noodle-bar chains are staking their claims along the coasts.

Last year, the first two stateside versions of London's Wagamama chain opened in the Boston area, and more are planned for the East Coast. Wagamama, with 80 eateries in a dozen countries, features edgy decors, communal seating, multiple noodle options and entrees costing $9 to $14.

"The appeal of noodles is universal, no doubt about it," says Paul O'Farrell, chief operating officer. "We do a great family business because kids love noodles. Parents are becoming more conscious of what their kids are eating and are steering them clear of fast food."

The Zao Noodle Bar chain, founded in Palo Alto, Calif., a decade ago, now has six locations in the Pacific Northwest, and further expansion is planned. The original concept prominently featured Japanese-style noodles, but those have been dropped in favor of Westernized Asian street-food dishes with Thai, Vietnamese and Chinese influences. Top sellers: ginger-garlic chile chicken and prawns and Vietnamese rice noodles with protein toppings.

"The spice and aromatics are a little dumbed-down compared to what you would find in Asia," says CEO Matthew Baizer. "But we're fresh. We take the essences of Asian flavors and add them to reasonably priced American dishes, and it has worked."

Another concept on the horizon is the Japanese izakaya. These rustic neighborhood taverns feature small plates of food that range from steamed edamame and other bar snacks to sushi, tempura and grilled-meat skewers. Most dishes are designed to be shared, and prices generally are lower than those in more formal Japanese restaurants.

Casual, independently owned versions already have strong footholds in areas with large Japanese populations, such as New York and the San Francisco Bay Area, but chain versions with more varied and upscale food options may not be far off: Two successful izakaya franchises in Japan have opened versions in Seattle (Wann Izakaya) and Los Angeles (Torafuku).

More significantly, the U.S. company that created the national chain of P. F. Chang's China Bistro restaurants has tested the waters in Scottsdale, Ariz., with an izakaya-inspired concept called Taneko Japanese Tavern. The menu, which incorporates organic and seasonal ingredients, embraces several Japanese cooking styles and East-West hybrid dishes such as Kobe beef burgers and tempura fish and chips.

"The idea was to take the comfort aspects of American taverns and Japanese taverns and produce an izakaya," says Rick Federico, CEO of P. F. Chang's China Bistro. Though Federico says Taneko has been successful during its two-year run, it hasn't generated the high-volume business the company requires to launch it as a national chain. P. F. Chang's is selling a majority of its stake in Taneko back to the founding parties, who may try to tweak the approach.

"Taneko may have been a little early into the marketplace, but these types of restaurants will become increasingly popular," Federico says. "They offer new and interesting flavor profiles, and U.S. consumers are much more adventuresome than they were 10 years ago."

—Jerry Shriver

Thai food such as this chicken red curry soup is often quite spicy.

Southeast Asia includes Thailand, Vietnam, Cambodia, Laos, Indonesia, Malaysia, and the Philippines. Chefs from this region often use fish sauce, lemongrass, and tamarind to flavor their dishes. They make sauces from coconut milk. Southeast Asian curries are usually a blend of different spices and citrus fruits. Foods are usually steamed or lightly stir-fried. Rice, vegetables, and fish are the mainstays.

ISLAND FLAVORS

For most of their history, Hawaiian men and women ate separately. This practice was part of Hawaiian religious beliefs. In 1819 King Kamehameha II of Hawaii created the luau. This large feast featured traditional Hawaiian food, music, and dance. At the luau, the king allowed men and women to eat together, ending the ancient practice of eating separately. In modern times, Hawaiians still hold luaus on special occasions. The menu always includes a whole roasted pig.

Modern Hawaiians have created a new style of cooking called Hawaiian regional cuisine. This style blends Japanese, Chinese, Korean, Filipino, Pacific Island, and European flavors. Cooks prepare meals using Hawaii's freshest local ingredients, including pineapples, oranges, and fish.

CHOPSTICKS, FINGERS, OR FORK AND KNIFE?

In Southwest Asia, most people eat with their fingers. This practice adds to the eating experience. People can feel the heat and the texture of what they are putting in their mouths. Their fingers are almost like extra tongues. In the United States, some Southwest

Master Chef Martin Yan

Martin Yan *(left)* is probably the most famous Chinese chef in the world. Yan was born in Guangzhou, a city in southern China. As a child, Yan was surrounded by food and cooking. His father owned a restaurant, and his mother owned a grocery store. By the age of thirteen, Yan was already cooking at a popular restaurant in Hong Kong. He studied cooking at the Overseas Institute of Cookery in Hong Kong. He then got a master's degree in food science from the University of California–Davis.

In 1978 he started his own television show. Called *Yan Can Cook*, the popular cooking show still airs around the world. Yan shares his recipes and cooking techniques in print too. He has written thirty cookbooks.

Many Asian Americans prefer eating with chopsticks rather than forks and knives.

Asian immigrants eat with their fingers. Others use forks and knives.

In China, Japan, Korea, and Vietnam, most people eat with chopsticks. No one knows who invented chopsticks, but they have been around for about five thousand years. Modern chopsticks are usually made

Recycling Chopsticks

Most chopsticks are made from wood, so making chopsticks requires cutting down trees. In China alone, loggers cut down twenty-seven million trees every year just to make chopsticks. After people eat with wooden chopsticks, they usually throw them away. This situation hurts the environment. First, used chopsticks pile up in landfills with other garbage. Second, trees are cut down to make chopsticks faster than new trees can grow. Some people have started to use metal and plastic chopsticks instead of wooden ones. People wash the sticks and use them again and again. In San Francisco's Japantown, one environmental group recycles wooden chopsticks. They use the sticks to make sculptures.

from bamboo or plastic. In the United States, many Asian immigrants eat with chopsticks. Most Asian American restaurants give customers a choice of chopsticks or forks and knives.

AMERICANIZATION OF ASIAN COOKING

Asian restaurants are found in every large city and many small towns across the United States. Getting Chinese takeout is as American as eating popcorn at the movie theater. Sushi has become an American favorite. Sushi is served in Japanese restaurants and at special "sushi bars." Even mainstream U.S. grocery stores carry packaged sushi.

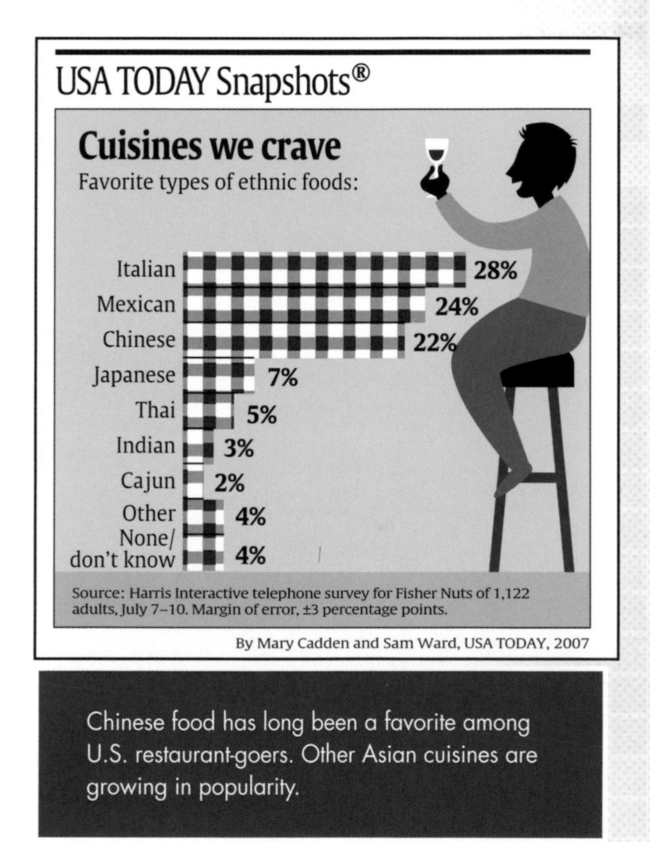

Chinese food has long been a favorite among U.S. restaurant-goers. Other Asian cuisines are growing in popularity.

But the Asian food served in Asian American restaurants is sometimes different from the food served in Asia. In fact, some menu items aren't even served in Asia. Asian American chefs created them to suit the tastes of Americans. Chop suey, General Tso's chicken, chow mein, and fortune cookies are examples of Chinese American foods that are not served in China.

Chicken Massaman Curry

This dish was introduced into southern and central Thailand from India. The Thai have added their own touches and have transformed it into a distinctive and special Thai curry. You can ask an adult for help with this recipe.

INGREDIENTS

8 chicken thighs or legs, skinned, boned, and cut into bite-size pieces
½ teaspoon salt
1 teaspoon garam masala
¼ teaspoon ground cardamom
1 stalk lemongrass, finely chopped, or 1 tablespoon dried lemongrass, soaked
3 tablespoons vegetable oil
1 2-inch stick cinnamon, or 1 teaspoon ground cinnamon
1 medium onion, peeled and cut into bite-size pieces
2 medium potatoes, peeled and cut into bite-size pieces
2 cups coconut milk
2 bay leaves
1 teaspoon sugar
2 tablespoons fish sauce
1 teaspoon lemon juice
¼ teaspoon crushed red pepper flakes
½ cup roasted peanuts, for garnish

PREPARATION

1. In a large bowl, mix chicken, salt, garam masala, cardamom, and lemongrass.
2. Heat the oil in a large skillet over medium-high heat. Add the cinnamon and onion, and fry about 5 minutes, or until onion turns brown. Add the chicken mixture and fry, stirring constantly, until chicken is brown.
3. Add potatoes, coconut milk, and bay leaves and stir. Cover, reduce heat to low, and simmer for 20 minutes, or until potatoes are tender.
4. Add sugar, fish sauce, lemon juice, and crushed red pepper flakes. Stir and cook for about 5 minutes to heat through.
5. Remove cinnamon stick and bay leaves from skillet. Serve with rice and garnish with peanuts.

Serves 4 to 6

As more Asians have immigrated to the United States, Americans have started to learn about different kinds of Asian food. Thai, Korean, and Vietnamese restaurants have become popular. Many cities have pan-Asian restaurants. These restaurants offer a blend of cooking traditions from across Asia. They are also known as fusion-style restaurants.

FAMOUS ASIAN PACIFIC AMERICANS

Keiko Agena (b. 1973)

Japanese American actress Keiko Agena was born in Honolulu, Hawaii. She started acting in theater at the age of ten. She has appeared in several popular television series, including *ER*, *Law and Order*, *Felicity*, and *Without a Trace*. She also played the role of Lane Kim on the show *Gilmore Girls*. In 2007 she won an Ammy Award for Best Female Actor in a Television Series for her role on *Felicity*. Ammys are like the Emmy Awards but are presented to only Asian American actors. In 2007 *People* magazine voted Agena one of the one hundred most beautiful people in the world. She played Private Hamamori in the 2008 movie *Major Movie Star*. When Agena is not acting, she likes riding her motorcycle.

Lynda Barry (b. 1956)

Lynda Barry is a Filipino, Irish, and Norwegian American author and cartoonist. As a child, she loved to draw, but she didn't sketch her first cartoon until she was in college. Her most famous cartoon is *Ernie Pook's Comeek*, which features a family of characters including sisters Marlys and Maybonne. She has also written illustrated novels, including *The Good Times Are Killing Me*, *Cruddy*, and *What It Is*. Born in Richland Center, Wisconsin, Barry attended college in Washington State. She later returned to southern Wisconsin, where she lives with her husband.

Benjamin Cayetano (b. 1939)

Born in Honolulu, Hawaii, Benjamin Cayetano was governor of Hawaii from 1994 to 2002. He is the first Filipino American to serve as a governor in the United States. Cayetano grew up in a rough neighborhood of Honolulu. When he was six years old, his parents divorced. He was raised by his father, an immigrant from the Philippines. After marrying and having children, Cayetano moved to Los Angeles to attend college. He graduated from the University of California–Los Angeles in 1968 and three years later from Loyola University School of Law in California. He and his family returned to Hawaii, where Cayetano became a trial attorney. Soon afterward, in 1974, he was elected to the Hawaii State Legislature. He then served as lieutenant governor of Hawaii before being elected governor. As governor, he is most remembered for his improvements in education. In 2009 Cayetano released his memoir, *Ben: A Memoir, from Street Kid to Governor*.

Ann Curry (b. 1956)

Since 1997, Ann Curry has said good morning to millions of viewers on NBC's *Today*. She has also hosted *Dateline NBC* since 2005. Curry's parents met at the end of World War II, when U.S. forces occupied Japan. Her father, in the U.S. Navy, was of mixed European and Cherokee descent. Her mother was Japanese. Curry was born in Guam, a U.S. territory in the Pacific. Because of her father's career in the navy, Ann and her family moved around a lot. She grew up in California, Virginia, and Oregon. She got a degree in journalism from the University of Oregon in 1978.

Danny Graves (b. 1973)

Danny Graves is a Major League Baseball pitcher. He was born toward the end of the Vietnam War in Ho Chi Minh City, Vietnam. His father was a U.S. serviceman. His Vietnamese mother worked for the U.S. Embassy in South Vietnam. Just before the end of the war, the family moved to Florida, where Graves took an interest in baseball. His talent as a pitcher earned him a scholarship to the University of Miami. He has pitched for the Cleveland Indians, the Cincinnati Reds, and the New York Mets. Graves is the first and only player born in Vietnam to play in Major League Baseball in the United States. In 2009 he and his mother made their first return trip to Vietnam. They were part of Bringing Baseball to Vietnam, a group working to make the sport popular in the country.

Bobby Jindal (b. 1971)

Piyush "Bobby" Jindal is an Asian Indian American and governor of Louisiana. His parents immigrated to the United States from India in 1970. As a child, Jindal was a fan of the TV show *The Brady Bunch*. He adopted the name Bobby because he identified with the character of the same name on the show. In high school, he converted from Hinduism to Catholicism. He earned degrees from Brown University in Rhode Island and Oxford University in the United Kingdom. After graduating, he was appointed to head Louisiana's Department of Health. In 1999 he became president of the University of Louisiana System. In 2001 President George W. Bush nominated him to be an adviser to the U.S. secretary of health and human services. In 2003 Jindal ran for governor of Louisiana but lost. Louisianans elected him to the U.S. House of Representatives in 2004, making him the second Asian Indian to serve in the U.S. Congress. Jindal was reelected to Congress in 2006 and became governor of Louisiana in 2007.

EXPLORE YOUR HERITAGE

Where did your family come from? Who are your relatives, and where do they live? Were they born in the United States? If not, when and why did they come here? Where did you get your family name? Is it German? Puerto Rican? Vietnamese? Something else? If you are adopted, what is your adoptive family's story?

By searching for the answers to these questions, you can begin to discover your family's history. And if your family history is hard to trace, team up with a friend to share ideas or to learn more about that person's family history.

Where to Start

Start with what you know. In a notebook or on your family's computer, write down the full names of the relatives you know about and anything you know about them—where they lived, what they liked to do as children, any awards or honors they earned, and so on.

Next, gather some primary sources. Primary sources are the records and observations of eyewitnesses to events. They include diaries; letters; autobiographies; speeches; newspapers; birth, marriage, and death records; photographs; and ship records. The best primary resources about your family may be in family scrapbooks or files in your home or in your relatives' homes. You may also find some interesting material in libraries, archives, historical societies, and museums. These organizations often have primary sources available online.

The Next Steps

After taking notes and gathering primary sources, think about what facts and details you are missing. You can then prepare to interview your relatives to see if they can fill in these gaps. First, write down any questions that you would like to ask them about their lives. Then ask your relatives if they would mind being interviewed. Don't be upset if they say no. Understand that some people do not like to talk about their pasts.

Also, consider interviewing family friends. They can often provide interesting stories and details about your relatives. They might have photographs too.

Family Interviews

When you are ready for an interview, gather your questions, a notepad, a tape recorder or camcorder, and any other materials you might need. Consider showing your interview subjects a photograph or a timetable of important events at the start of your interview. These items can help jog the memory of your subjects and get them talking. You might also bring U.S. and world maps to an interview. Ask your subjects to label the places they have lived.

Remember that people's memories aren't always accurate. Sometimes they forget information and confuse dates. You might want to take a trip to the library or look online to check dates and other facts.

Get Organized!

When you finish your interviews and research, you are ready to organize your information. There are many ways of doing this. You can write a history of your entire family or individual biographies of your relatives. You can create a timeline going back to your earliest known ancestors. You can make a family tree—a diagram or chart that shows how people in your family are related to one another.

If you have collected a lot of photographs, consider compiling a photo album or scrapbook that tells your family history. Or if you used a camcorder to record your interviews, you might even want to make a movie.

However you put together your family history, be sure to share it! Your relatives will want to see all the information you found. You might want to create a website or blog so that other people can learn about your family. Whatever you choose to do, you'll end up with something your family will appreciate for years to come.

ASIAN PACIFIC AMERICAN SNAPSHOT

This chart gives a statistical snapshot of five Asian American groups living in the United States. It looks at how many Asian Americans from each group are living in the country and which states have the greatest populations. All figures are based on individuals claiming full or partial ancestry in the designated Asian American group in the 2000 U.S. Census.

ASIAN PACIFIC GROUP	TOTAL U.S. POPULATION	FIVE TOP STATES OF RESIDENCE	YEARS OF GREATEST IMMIGRATION
Chinese	**2,858,291**	California: 1,122,187 New York: 451,859 Hawaii: 170,803 Texas: 121,588 New Jersey: 110,263	1848–1885, 1970s to present
Filipino	**2,385,216**	California: 918,678 Hawaii: 170,635 Illinois: 86,298 New Jersey: 85,245 New York: 81,681	1903–1934, 1970s to present
Asian Indian	**1,855,590**	California: 314,819 New York: 251,724 New Jersey: 169,180 Texas: 129,365 Illinois: 124,723	1910s, 1950s, 1980s, 1995 to present
Korean	**1,226,825**	California: 345,882 New York: 119,846 New Jersey: 65,349 Illinois: 51,453 Washington: 46,880	1904–1910, 1950s, 1965 to present
Vietnamese	**1,212,465**	California: 447,032 Texas: 134,961 Washington: 46,149 Virginia: 37,309 Massachusetts: 33,962	1975 to present

GLOSSARY

Americanize: to adopt American customs and culture

character: a symbol used in some Asian writing. Most characters stand for parts of words or for ideas.

culture: the knowledge, values, behaviors, and beliefs shared by a group of people

discrimination: treating someone differently because of his or her ethnic background, race, religion, gender, or other factors

fluent: capable of using a language easily and accurately

immigrant: a person who moves from the country of his or her birth to another country

intern: to place people in confinement, especially during wartime

lunar calendar: a calendar based on the cycles of the moon. People use lunar calendars in many parts of Asia. The calendars differ from the solar calendar (based on the movements of the sun) used in the United States.

martial arts: ancient Asian fighting arts such as karate and kung fu

minority: a part of a population differing from mainstream culture in some characteristics and often subjected to different or unfair treatment

monastery: a home for people who have devoted their lives to religious worship

mosque: a Muslim place of worship

pan-Asian: spanning the continent of Asia

refugee camp: an area providing shelter to people who have left their home because of war, political unrest, or persecution

temple: a place of worship

SOURCE NOTES

21 Internet Movie Database, "Biography for Ang Lee," Internet Movie Database, 2009, http://www.imdb.com/name/nm0000487/bio (September 14, 2009).

26 Kai-Ming Cha, "The First Asian American Comicon Is a Cool Success," *Publisher's Weekly*, July 14, 2009, http://www.publishersweekly.com/article/CA6670757.html (August 19, 2009).

34 Jaymes Song, "Wie Has Woods' Marketability," *Honolulu Star Bulletin*, October 6, 2005, http://archives.starbulletin.com/2005/10/06/sports/story03.html (August 19, 2009).

SELECTED BIBLIOGRAPHY

Cao, Lan, and Himilce Novas. *Everything You Need to Know about Asian-American History*. New York: Plume, 1996.
This title gives a history of some of the largest Asian American groups in the United States. Each chapter is laid out in a question-and-answer format. The book covers early laws affecting Asian immigrants, discrimination, and current issues.

Dudley, William, ed. *Asian Americans: Opposing Viewpoints*. San Diego: Greenhaven Press, 1996.
This title offers a collection of essays about the Asian American experience throughout history.

Gong, Rosemary. *Good Luck Life: The Essential Guide to Chinese American Celebrations and Culture*. New York: HarperCollins Publishers, 2005.
Written by a Chinese American, this book describes in detail important Chinese American celebrations and the history behind them.

Hu, Brian, and Ada Tseng. "APA Top Ten: Non-Asian Themed Movies Directed by Asian Americans." *Asia Pacific Arts*, UCLA Asia Institute, September 19, 2008. http://www.asiaarts.ucla.edu/080919/article.asp?parentID=97605 (March 21, 2009).
This article provides in-depth reviews of movies made by Asian Americans for a mainstream audience.

Lott, M. Ray. *The American Martial Arts Film*. Jefferson, NC: McFarland & Company, 2004.
This book offers a history and critique of American-made martial arts films. The book also describes martial arts in the United States.

Merin, Melody. "Asian Americans First Won Olympic Gold 60 Years Ago." America.gov, May 30, 2008. http://www.america.gov/st/sports-english/2008/May/20080530165620xlrennef0.5189478.html (March 22, 2009).
This article describes some of the difficulties early Asian American athletes had to face to compete for the United States in the Olympics.

U.S. Bureau of the Census. *"We the People: Asians in the United States."* Census 2000 Special Reports. Prepared by Terrance J. Reeves and Claudette E. Bennett in the Racial Statistics Branch, Bureau of the Census, 2004.
This report provides a detailed analysis of the 2000 U.S. Census material about Asian Americans.

FURTHER READING AND WEBSITES

Asiafood.com
http://www.asiafood.com
This website features recipes, articles about Asian food, and more.

Asian-Nation: Asian American History, Demographics, and Issues
http://www.asian-nation.org
This website provides historical and current information about Asian American culture.

Hirahara, Naomi. *1001 Cranes*. New York: Delacorte, 2008.
A Japanese American girl goes to live with her grandparents while her parents are going through a divorce. Although she dreads the move, she learns much about herself and Japanese culture.

In America series. Minneapolis: Lerner Publications Company, 2005–2006.
This series features several titles on Asian Americans, including Pakistanis, Koreans, Chinese, East Indians, Vietnamese, and Filipinos in America. Each book examines one ethnic group's immigrant experience up close.

Levy, Debbie. *The Vietnam War*. Minneapolis: Twenty-First Century Books, 2004.
Readers can get information about the Vietnam War from a brief description of the region's history and the U.S. involvement in the conflict.

Millet, Sandra. *The Hmong of Southeast Asia*. Minneapolis: Lerner Publications Company, 2002.
A title in the First Peoples series, this book looks closely at the culture of the Hmong, one of the earliest Asian peoples.

Nguyen, Chi, and Judy Monroe. *Cooking the Vietnamese Way*. Minneapolis: Lerner Publications Company, 2002.
This is one of several Asian titles in the Easy Menu Ethnic Cookbook series. Others cover Indian, Chinese, Indonesian, Japanese, Korean, and Thai cooking. Each book briefly covers the country's history and geography. The menus are easy to prepare. Most ingredients are available in grocery stores.

Ollhoff, Jim. *Martial Arts Movies*. Edina, MN: ABDO & Daughters, 2008.
Part of the World of Martial Arts series, this book discusses some of the most popular martial arts films in history.

Sakurai, Gail. *Asian-Americans in the Old West*. New York: Children's Press, 2000.
This title takes a close look at the challenges and hardships Asian immigrants to the United States faced in the 1800s.

Singh Mann, Gurinder, Paul David Numrich, and Raymond B. Williams. *Buddhists, Hindus, and Sikhs in America*. New York: Oxford University Press, 2001.
This book looks at the history of three Asian religious groups in the United States, including the prejudices that followers still face.

Sinnott, Susan. *Extraordinary Asian Americans and Pacific Islanders*. New York: Children's Press, 2003.
The author provides short biographies of dozens of outstanding Asian Americans.

Visual Geography Series. Minneapolis: Twenty-first Century Books, 2003–2011.
Each book in this series explains the land, history, government, people, culture, and economy of a different nation. The series includes titles on Bangladesh, China, India, Japan, Laos, Pakistan, Thailand, Vietnam and more. Readers may also visit http://www.vgsbooks.com, the home page of the series, for late-breaking news and statistics.

INDEX

PHOTO ACKNOWLEDGMENTS

The images in this book are used with the permission of: © Robert Deutsch/USA TODAY, pp. 3 (top), 7, 14 (top); © Jack Gruber/USA TODAY, pp. 3 (second from top), 8, 12; © Robert Hanashiro/USA TODAY, pp. 3 (third from top) 23, 31, 34 (top); © USA TODAY, pp. 3 (forth from top), 32 (both), 35, 44; © Ian Cumming/Axiom Photographic Agency/ Getty Images, pp. 3 (third from bottom), 46 (left); © Susana Bates/ZUMA Press, pp. 3 (second from bottom), 50; © iStockphoto.com/Julie Kaptelova, pp. 3 (bottom), 66; © Rich Iwasaki/Alamy, p. 4; California Historical Society (FN-25345), p. 6 (top); courtesy of Kao Kalia Yang, photo by Der Yang, p. 14 (bottom); Buena Vista/Hollywood/The Kobal Collection, p. 16; © Otto Dyar/John Kobal Foundation/Getty Images, p. 17; Universal/The Kobal Collection, p. 18; © Fotos International/Archive Fotos/Getty Images, p. 20; Everett Collection/Rex Features USA, p. 21; © Jason Merritt/Getty Images, p. 22 (both); © Todd Plitt/USA TODAY, pp. 24, 58; © New Vision Technologies, Inc/Digital Vision/Getty Images, p. 25; © Luigi Novi/Nightscream, p. 26; © James P. Blair/National Geographic/Getty Images, p. 27; © Matthew Stockman/Getty Images, p. 30; AP Photo/Ronen Zilberman, pp. 33, 70 (bottom); © David Cannon/Getty Images, p. 34 (bottom); © Ed Clark/Time Life Pictures/Getty Images, p. 36; © Rex Hardy Jr./Time Life Pictures/Getty Images, p. 37 (top); © LWA/Photographers Choice/Getty Images, p. 37 (bottom); © Joe Sohm/Visions for America, LLC/Alamy, p. 40; © Paul D. Slaughter/Photographer's Choice/Getty Images, p. 41; © Michael Ventura/Alamy, p. 42; © Jeff Greenberg/Alamy, p. 43; © Kim Steele/Taxi/ Getty Images, p. 46 (right); © Mario Tama/Getty Images, p. 48; © Frances Roberts/Alamy, p. 49; © iStockphoto.com/Digitalskillet, p. 51; © Lynnette Peizer/Alamy, p. 52; © Gary Coronado/ZUMA Press, p. 54; © Kathleen Voege/Getty Images, p. 56; © Tim Dillon/USA TODAY, pp. 57, 60; © Joe Gough/Dreamstime.com, p. 59; © iStockphoto. com/Joakim Leroy, p. 64; © Craig Lee/San Francisco Chronicle/CORBIS, p. 65; Jim Smeal/ Beiimages/Rex Features USA, p. 70 (top); © Darron Fick, p. 70 (center); © Gregory Pace/ CORBIS, p. 71 (top); © Marc Serota/Getty Images, p. 71 (center); © Gannett News Service, Heather Wines/USA TODAY, p. 71 (bottom).

Front cover: © Susana Bates/ZUMA Press (top); © Rick Shupper/Ambient Images, Inc./ Alamy (bottom left); © iStockphoto.com/Daniel Loiselle (bottom right).

ABOUT THE AUTHOR

Karen Sirvaitis is a freelance writer and editor. She has written more than twenty books. She lives in northwestern Wisconsin with her family.